PLAGUE POEMS:
2020 Vision

by
Richard Harteis

Poets' Choice Publishing

Copyright © 2020 Poets' Choice Publishing
All rights reserved
Printed in the United States of America

Graphic Design: Barbara Shaw
Dawley paintings photos: Sue Parish

Library of Congress Cataloging-in-Publication Data pending
ISBN 978-1-7335400-6-3

Poets' Choice Publishing
337 Kitemaug Road
Uncasville, CT 06382
Poets-Choice.com

for Roger and Sara

Contents

Acknowledgments • vii
Prologue • viii
Days of Restriction • x

PANDEMIC
    Red Face • 2
    Camus Redux • 3
    Grandmother's Lament • 4
    Grace • 5
    Peony 1 • 7
    Encounter • 8
    Secrets Fathers Have Told Me • 9
    Laboratory • 10
    Peony 2 • 11
    Dream Journal • 12
    Visitation Four • 13
    Transfiguration • 15
    Alphabet Soup • 16
    Orange Face • 17
    Herd Immunity • 18
    Crow • 19

PLAY
    Work in Progress • 22
    The Nursery Wars • 23
    First Son • 24
    Birthday Boy • 25
    Pandemic Advice • 26
    Fractured Fairy Tales • 27
    Fish • 28
    Disaster on the Charles • 29
    Birds in a Row • 30
    Star Chamber • 31
    Orpheus Explains Calais to Apollo • 32
    Condomdrum • 33

Side by Side • 34
For a Serbian Friend • 35
Summer • 36
Post Prandial Two • 38
Birthday Party: July 3, 2020 • 39
Treasure Hunting, He Thinks of Selling • 40
Salvo • 41
Summer Lantern. • 42

ROOM MATE
Pepperoni • 47
Living with Stanley Kowalski • 48
Lily Petals • 49
Lost • 50
After Frost • 51
Peony 3 • 52
Last Shift • 53
Covid Casualty • 54

EASTER
Stretching Out • 58
Post Prandial • 59
Palm Sunday • 60
Peony 4 • 61
Easter: 4:00 AM • 62
The Good Old Days • 63
Saturday, Holy Week • 64

EPILOGUE
Face • 68
Camus' Stranger. • 697

ABOUT THE ARTISTS • 71
White Lotus • 73

All titles which are italicized are paintings by Rita Dawley
Peony Series and final image: Juner Patnode

Acknowledgments

Pancho Malenzanov

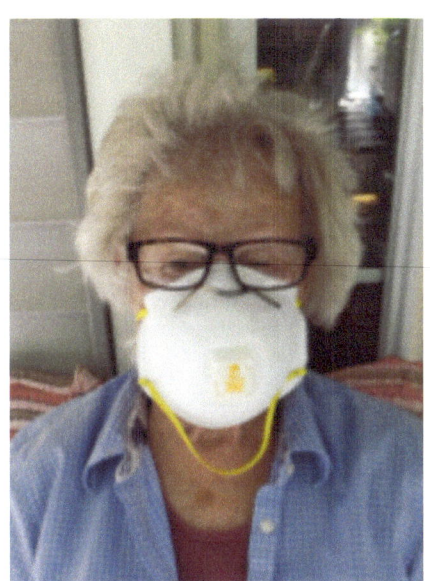

Rita Dawley

Yujuan Zhai - Juner Patnode
Photo credit: Vincent Scarano

Prologue

"It ain't over 'til it's over," I believe the great Yogi said. To which someone added, "yeah but when it's over, it's over." Well, who knows what the future will bring? Que sera sera. We may be facing a very dark winter as in Game of Thrones, or we will see the death of this virus at the kind hands of nature who so unkindly delivered it to us in 2020.

Like other artists in this pandemic, I have struggled to come to terms with all the new burdens it has brought us: masks, social distancing, shortages, less than truthful politicians and scientists, loneliness, fear, sexual frustration and the sad irony of putting all this in the context of a beautiful spring and creatures not knowing the world has changed. A woodpecker rat tat tapping on a tree in the forest for his breakfast, puffs of daisy seeds flowing on the breeze, the sun so warm, the grass so green and fresh. Robins, titmouse, and tiny hummingbirds miraculously making their way across the Gulf for a little bit of sugar water in burgeoning blossoms.

It is a world Camus first looked at in his book THE PLAGUE and another, THE STRANGER. His words become prologue and epilogue to my own observations, and in the middle of all of this so far, the season of Easter with its promise of resurrection and transformation. Love, amusement, hope and just training your mind to observe what the world has become and what it may yet be, the opportunities Camus first looked at in his plague and later The Stranger.

One happy result of this artistic thrashing about has been the chance to reconnect with old friends such as Pancho Malenzanov who painted his village in the middle of a hurricane which seems appropriate for the cover of this particular book. And today I'll meet Mark Patnode's new bride, Juner who has come from China and has painted beautiful images of flowers, a kind of new infection of beauty which will grace these poems. It's become a kind of trademark for Poets Choice to include the visual arts with the written, one art form en-hancing the other, lending strength to the finished product. Ironic and lovely if this Chinese woman can bring some joy and beauty into our world. The soft, somewhat romantic images harmonize with the surrealistic paintings, sometimes humorous, sometimes severe, even disturbing which our local shaman, Rita Dawley has created as a response to the pandemic.

I divided the book into four parts, somewhat arbitrarily beginning with Pandemic; then Play including occasional observations and attempts at humor; then Roommate, since when you're living with someone you get to learn a lot about them; and—finally—Easter with prayers to help us see the light. "Covid Casualty" is a sad reflection on the aftermath of living in lockdown with someone you love, a drama which has played out in any number of households as the isolation and forced togetherness takes its toll. A sacrilege perhaps to compare the suffocation of a roommate who could not breathe to that of George Floyd dying at the hands of a cruel fellow human being, and the global uproar fueled by the frustrations of isolation. A single poem serves as an epilogue, since its rather bleak assessment does not really suit for the section titled Easter. Still, as an indictment of capital punishment, it seems an appropriate vision of Camus' humanism, his compassion for the human predicament to end with. As da Vinci has said "it is an infinitely atrocious act to take away the life of a man." This is what the virus has done atrociously in thousands of cases now. These poems mean nothing if they forget those thousands who in desperation and courage have achieved their own death. The collection ends with a final image of hope and resurrection, a last final word. Even when its roots are in the dirtiest waters, the lotus produces the most beautiful flower, an ancient symbol of rebirth, purity and self regeneration. It calls for spiritual enlightenment so direly needed in these troubling times when all life is threatened.

Days of Restriction

Pandemic

Red face

Camus Redux

"The plague bacillus never dies or vanishes entirely,…it can remain dormant for dozens of years in furniture or clothing,…it waits patiently in bedrooms, cellars, trunks, handkerchiefs and old papers, and…perhaps the day will come when for the instruction or misfortune of mankind, the plague will rouse its rats and send them to die in some well-contented city."

Albert Camus, The Plague

Like New York. Hitler dead, Mussolini gone,
Petain in the ash can of history.
But the rats are out again,
Nova virus, Nova Fascism. Can we muster
the compassion Camus felt in the middle of it
All, his sympathy for humanity, (at the risk of
Turning evil into a banality as Hannah Arendt
Would have it.) Disease, separation and exile
Come upon us unexpectedly, absurdly, and
The only way to fight the plague is with
Decency, Camus tells us. But how can we not
Blame our country now, left and right.
How can we find the will to resist
Compromise, to survive, to love?

Grandmother's Lament

Everyone is in such a dither
Over this Povid 19 or whatever
They call it. Went to my favorite
Chinese take out this evening.
And everyone looked at me
Full of shame. Oh Lord, where
Will the fear go next?
It all comes to us
Regardless of race, creed or
Color as they say. We are all
Hanging out in the trees
With our babies clinging
To our breasts.

Grace

I

Katherine Hull was dancing with a Russian prince
And couldn't resist bragging a little about the lapis
Lazuli gracing her neck and bare shoulders.
Her hand floated like a dove above her chest.
"What do you think of my necklace" she asked him,
An admirer gave it to me some time ago…."

"It's lovely," he said, looking down finally,
"Mama had a staircase of it."

She smiled and simply kept on dancing
While every man in the room daydreamed
Of burying his face in those lovely breasts
Which rose and fell as he led her in the
Waltz under the brilliant stars of Capri.

She was young then, ripe. But
It was years before she could find it
Amusing enough to tell the story
Of the snarky prince at cocktails.

II

Pierre Teilhard de Chardin
Was drafted in WWI and offered
A commission. He chose instead
To be a stretcher bearer and let
That grizly work plant the seed
Of his vision of the cosmos, how
God enters into the physical
World, Peking Man to the
Omega Point: "The world is
Round so that friendship may
Encircle it."

There's no accounting really
For this beautiful ingénue, or
A priest working in the mud
In the fields of France.

Peony 1

Encounter

We walked under the cherry and dogwood
Blossoms and came across a young father
Trying to coax his adorable two year old
Into a stroller. The baby screamed on and on,
A real melt down. "He's been like this all
Day," the dad explained, embarrassed,
Exasperated.

"What's up little dude," I asked the baby.
He looked at me with curiosity for a minute
Then kept on wailing.
Blond hair, blue eyes
Like his adorable papa.
But the child's face
Just turned red and redder with boredom.

"Why are you at home," I asked the man
Standing under his dogwood tree.

"We're closed, you know. Pandemic. But,
I got certified today! Home repair. I can
Put in a furnace, or fix your dishwasher."

"That's us, I told him. We always need help.
We're all in this together. Congratulations!"

His face broke into a smile bright as
The spring sun. "Thanks," he said. But,

The baby kept it up somehow. I guess
That's what two year olds are about, they
Can't imagine anything else but themselves yet,
Like the President, they would rather just cry.

Secrets Fathers Have Told Me

I gave up a great professional opportunity
So my son could continue to play football.

I got him that job at the university and
He has no idea I pulled the strings.

It is a little hard on us all, but we have
Kept the baby, despite her palsy, in our home.

You have always been in My embrace
And will be from here to eternity.

This love, must, per force, remain anonymous.

Laboratory

Hope and fear, fear and hope
This is the human genius:
The spirit can accommodate
Both simultaneously. And so,
We muddle on in our bipolar way,
Hoping for some sort of clarity,
Fearing there's none to be had,
Swinging from one pole to the other,
Content with the cliché, "it is what it is, we are
who we are." Fight or flight, Flight or
Fight. We chose instead to
Play dead and let our little heart beat
As silently as possible. We're all just
Mice, looking for a little food,
Looking for a way out, oblivious
Of our sweet eyes, our silky backs
Asking Him for a little compassion.

Peony 2

Dream Journal
for Giulietta Masina

Last night I lived in La Strada.

It took some coaxing to keep six feet
Away from the master who bought me
From my mother. I only wanted love
Hanging there between the sky and earth,
Wide eyed, dreaming of the ocean.

But I had locked incisors with a black dog
Until I freed myself by biting off his nose. Still,
It didn't keep him from sniffing me out.
I could not break the chain from my breast
Like the brute for whom I played the trumpet.
I tossed and turned every time the dog came
In hot pursuit. There were no detours in
La Strada, no pope or priest to keep him
Off the trail until I woke to the world
And the smell of cappuccino and biscotti
To start yet another insomniac day.

Visitation Four

Tonight it is dinner with Lyubomir.
We've looked everywhere in the
Crowded restaurant, a Peruvian
Trattoria packed with jolly brown
Patrons, laughing, smoking, all
Talking at once, so packed, the
Waiter can barely navigate.

Lyubo is nowhere to be seen.
We're late, fairly frantic to
Find him because though he
will not show it, he will be mad.

"Out on the terrace," the maître d
Explains, and sure enough
Luybomir sits at the sole table
Shaded under a large umbrella,
Five salads waiting expectantly.

He smiles and stands to greet us.
Now the rakia can begin.

"How are you doing Richie,
Any new poems Georgi?"

We grow warm with the sun
And brandy flowing through
Our veins. Everything will
Be friendly, all right.

A yellow bird drops on the table,
Flown all the way from Africa
Looking for a piece of bread.
He holds Lyubomir's finger

With his tiny pink claws
Like a baby holding on for
Dear life. We all sit silent
Taken by his dear black eyes
And let the omen speak.

Transfiguration

It's said they linger with us
Forty days after their passing.
They dawdle among us, looking
In, in our time of need, reluctant
To leave the sweet earth,
Dragging their feet.

And so the dear ghost
Is with us still. Cannot, yet,
For the love of us, illuminate
Into His divinity on Tabor
Mountain and leave us
Looking heavenward
For afterward.

Alphabet Soup

She's added a new anagram
To her living will. DNR, for sure.
She doesn't want some eager young
EMT breaking all her ribs trying
To resuscitate her doing CPR.

But these days, she's not even
Comfortable with CPAP. So, DNV
Has been added in the middle of
The COVID-19 pandemic - Not
To be confused with the DMV.
Travel restrictions are already in
Place. She rarely goes out and has
No need of her HC license plate.

She's tested negative, this is
Only a pre-emptive decision.
But the old Gray Jacobik,
She 'ain't what she used to be.
So DNV, do not ventilate
Please, if the situation arises.
When her number's up,
All she wants is RIP. Resigned,
These days, instead of "Love,"
She signs her e-mails with "Alas."

Orange Face

Herd Immunity
For Karena

He: "Do you mind wearing a mask?"

She: "I don't need no motherfucking
Mask, motherfucker. I don't need
Some old bastard telling me
What to do. Fuck you."

Once infected, antibodies are
Supposed to kick in. But
The immunity
Is only temporary,
And the whole social house
Of cards begins to collapse.

The second wave
Is on its way.
Let the bitch have her fucking say.

Crow

There is a crow complaining in the yard,
Black thoughts in the green grass.
He makes his imitation duck noises
Like calling the hunters hiding in the blind.

Is he looking for a little aged road kill,
Or just hopping around letting the earthworms
Know an earthquake is about to occur.
Mostly, he just seems bored, normal crow attitude.

He'd like to know what we're thinking
Folded in each others arms when the sun
Has almost peaked overhead. He's not sure
He likes this leisure, the state of the world
As the globe slows it's spinning.

"Caw, caw." Time to rise and shine.

PLAY

Work in Progress

The Nursery Wars

> "They sacrifice every day
> for their children's furniture"
> —Donald Trump on Military Heroes.

Bam! Get that terrorist
Tracking his trundle bed.

Blow up the bitch
Busting his bassinet.

Move the tricycle
Into a safe house.

Camouflage the mobile
Daffy, Bugs and Daisy
All gone incognito.

Turn out the night light,
Strap on your night vision.

Semper Fidelis.
Over there, over there.

Colonel Bonespur
Wants a few good men.

First Son: Commiserating with the Baron

> "God's eye and a mother's love
> are all we're sure of in life."
> –Andrew Cuomo

Every teenager thinks their
parents are creepy or
embarrassing at some point.

But this poor kid is living with
POTUS and FLOTUS. Imagine his
Bad luck, and give him a little slack.

Birthday Boy, June 14

Not to be outdone, if he could raise her
from the dead, Marilyn would come
singing Happy Birthday to him. But
There are some things even he can't
Control yet, though he's working on it.

He'll just have to do with a hologram
Unless he dresses up Melania or one
Of his other women in sequins and have
A big party on Fox. Michelle Obama
Has another commitment, unfortunately.

Pandemic Advice from a Senile Friend

She's got the American
Version of "bats in the belfry":
Raccoons in the attic.
Medicare will pay for
A good neurologist,
(What pill can Melania give
her hubby for heart worm?)

But the exterminator comes
Out of pocket. Let him put
On a mask and gloves and
Trap them with peanut butter
Or whatever raccoons like
And put them out to pasture
In some other neighborhood.

Just don't let one of the rabid
Little bastard bandits bite you.
You don't want things to get
Any more complicated
Than they already are.

Fractured Fairy Tales

I
    Bo Peep Insouciant

I don't know where he went.
Probably out grazing, looking
For an unsuspecting ewe,
Some Yoe he could do the
Nasty with. Bam bam.
Baby ram lambs are like that.
What can you say, Bo Peep,
And Bo Play, too. Goes with
Herding. Boys aren't the only
Ones who can have fun
With sheep.

II
    The Spider Speaks Out

That Muffet chick is a weird bird.
All I did was sashay up to that pile
Of grass she was sitting on,
Friendly like, just to see
What she was eating.

Then boom, she was
Off social distancing big time
Like I was Godzilla or
Something. Could have knocked me
Over with a Feather.
Next time will be different.
I shoulda just bit the bitch.

Fish

Disaster on the Charles - 2009

"Aren't you afraid of the
Kepone in the river
Poisoning the fish,"
I ask the good old boy
Barbecuing the herring
During their spring run.

"All I gotta say," he says is
"Keep on
Eaten 'em."

Birds in a Row

Star Chamber on the First Floor of the Senior Housing Complex

Five or six old ladies sit like archbishops
Determining the fate of the building or
The culture or their blood pressure.
They aren't dressed in red,
But their authority is undeniable.

I avoid them when I can.

Orpheus Explains Calais to Apollo

"Orpheus had abstained from the love of women, either because things ended badly for him, or because he had sworn to do so. Yet, many felt a desire to be joined with the poet, and many grieved at rejection. Indeed, he was the first of the Thracian people to transfer his affection to young boys and enjoy their brief springtime, and early flowering this side of manhood."
 –Ovid, *The Metamorphoses,* Book X

"And Orpheus, the son of Thracian Oeagrus, loved Calais, the son of Boreas, with all his heart, and went often in shaded groves still singing of his desire, nor was his heart at rest. But always sleepless cares wasted his spirits as he looked at fresh Calais. The Bistonides, sharpening their long swords, ringed and killed him because he was the first in Thrace to desire men and disapprove the love of women."
 –Phanocles (c 225 B.C.)

I've had it with that Eurydice business, anyhow.

It was a terror for us both as we made our way
Through the darkness. She cried out, and I thought
She had stumbled or had turned an ankle.
I looked back, admittedly. Who knows what women
Really want? We are trained to love and
Protect them. An enigma. But she vanished
Like the ghost of love.

Now. I wander through the sacred grove
LikeNarcissus mesmerized by his own image and find
Calais sleeping underneath the oleander.
A perfect kouros, yes.* But
Look how long his eyelashes are, father,
his sleeping mouth fallen open, ripe,
as he lies lost in dream.

---

*A Kouros is the modern term given to free-standing Ancient Greek sculptures representing nude male youths. In Ancient Greek, Kouros means "youth, boy, especially of noble rank."

Condomdrum

If the invisible man raped her
Wouldn't his jizz be invisible too?
How can you crack an egg
With invisible jizz? Maybe she
Should put down her butcher
Knife and go along for the ride.

"You realize young lady, that
Rape means forced
Penetration," The judge
Remonstrated her
In the witness box.

"Yep, that's how it was,
Your honor. It was just rape
Rape rape, all night long."

Side By Side

For a Serbian Friend

Each of us
Carries a target
On our back.

When they hit you,
Miloševic; me, Clinton.

How sweet it would be
To throw our jackets
Into the fire, and run
Like naked Children
On a green field,
In spring, hand in hand.

Summer

Daddy had an orange run about
With white leather seats and
Twin Mercury engines, a poor
Man's Ferrari, skimming along
The Susquehanna or putting in
On the bay to go crabbing or fishing
For electric ells among the grasses.
The crab's blue pincers
Held tighter to the chicken necks
Than the clenched teeth of a pit bull .

We'd pull them up gingerly and
Drop them into a bucket for
Steaming and Wooden mallets
Later at the end of the day
When we returned, sunburned,
Thirsty for a cold Yuengling and
After, maybe, some Monopoly. Once,
Someone spilled the bucket and
We all went screaming with joy
Trying to get the blue monsters
Out from under the couch.
Even the dog got into the picture.

Sometimes my teenage boyfriend
Would join us. "How you liking it
So far," my dad would call from the
Front of the boat. We'd never had
The time for training, didn't know
The difference between fore and aft.

Only years later, when I finally had
The courage to kiss him, did Peggy Lee's
Immortal words come back to me:
Chicks were meant to give you beaver.
Guys were meant to get you laid.

But then it was summer, all was
Only potential, and hunger pulled us
Gently from the murky bottom
Of life to love's bright future.

Post Prandial Two

Earlier in the late spring
The white arms reaching
For the sky seemed like old men.

This evening, mid May, they are
A group of Sylphs whose slender
Fingers reach for the sky but at their
Tips are painted brilliantly red.

Birthday Party: July 3, 2020

Colonel Bonespur glides in Over Mount Rushmore
Like a Klingon General Flexing his wings.
The MAGA Pterodactyl, Red white and blue,
Blocks ou the sun while The adoring masses lift
Their eyes and salute him. They've come goose stepping
Across America to greet Commander Death, his words
Falling like black rain from heaven to drown out any dissent
From the zombie herd staggering toward November.

Treasure Hunting, He Thinks of Selling

Back again. A great tree has fallen
In the Southern corner where
William's ashes are buried.

I find the small toy my father gave me:
A stuffed tiger with green glass eyes,
The tail stitched between his legs,
The way a father might explain anatomy
To a baby. "Yes that is part of you, son!"

Some strange ghost-like creatures
Strutting across a Haitian field
Like chickens in a painting I brought
Home one year—walking on the wall.

And my sweet dog, scratching herself
Because the spring grasses have let
The fleas jump up on her as she ran
Like the proverbial wind through the fields.

Then comes a moment when the sky
And river are equally lavender
Against the primavera April fields.

Too many things to mention,
I will simply have to
Bury my heart here.

Salvo

There's a turkey, a big boy,
Though he hasn't fanned himself
Out yet, who runs back and forth
Back and forth along the fence

Looking for a mate, just
Pissed that he can't get to
The other side? He is me,
Of course, in this age of
Social distancing. Us all.

Sweet master turkey,
Deal with it. Keep running,
Even against a fence.
We all have to face
Something. Hang in
There brother turkey.

Summer Lantern
for Andrew

I

Here at Senior Housing,
The first firefly of summer
Sets off his torch over the field.
Love love love, electric on the
Night, and at the edge of the field,
A little Bambi with white spots,
About the tiniest deer ever,
Hanging out with her mother
Until she sees me and high tails it,
Not fully white yet, into the forest.

When we were children, grown Bambi's,
We would crouch underneath the fireflies
To see them against the evening sky and
Flapped them down, blinking there
In the grass to put into a bottle with
Holes at the top and a little grass
to make a summer lantern.

II

This virus has slapped me down.
I'm in a jar blinking with all the other
Old people, remembering summer,
What it has been and what may yet be
With the first firefly of summer.

III

Earlier in the day I worked with a
Young man who was very strong, and
Self-assured to organize my library.
I watched the sinews in his legs and
Perfect peapod buttox as he bent to
Shift his weight into a bookcase and
Make it fit, by God, into the empty space.

IV

Outside my window, Julia, the deer who
Comes every summer to eat green apples,
Who still grazes on her piano-string
Ligaments in those impossibly fragile legs
To carry her into the bush full speed.

I am indoors with my library helper
Whose beautiful arms and legs are
Turning this room into a possible space.
He throws himself into it, gets up a
Sweet sweat to lift up my spirit
The way only a Bambi or a beautiful
Fellow, or a firefly can do.

Room Mate

Pepperoni

Whenever it's on sale
Which is always, Mikey buys
One bag of pepperoni so
He can get the second one free.
When you open the dangerous
Door of our refrigerator now
Bags of pepperoni fall out
Like frogs from heaven. "It isn't
A bargain if you don't need it,"
My dad always said. How much Pepperoni
Two can two guys and a dog eat?

"I'll go to the bank and get wine
And salmon for tonight's party,"
I text Mikey. "And shrimp,"
He texts back. In the immortal words of
Mick Jagger, "You can't always get What
You want," Mikey. "You get what You
Need." But you are sweet and a
Nor'easter is about to blow down on us. I
Guess we need shrimp.
And maybe some pepperoni.

Living with Stanley Kowalski

He is a little broken,
Or compromised at least.
Not playing with a full deck
As they say. But who
Among us wins all the
Time in life's Black Jack.

Everybody's afraid of something -
The dark, bridges, living alone,
A claustrophobic mind.

He's beautiful, like Billy Budd.
And can not speak up for himself.
He rebuffs all effort to have him be
A younger brother or a lover. Others
Have told him he can not be a
Contender. And the pity is that he
Believes them, standing there in
The spring evening with his dark
Eyes and broad shoulders, Trying to
Make sense of it like a flower
Gleaming in the rain.

Lily Petals

White and translucent as
Silk or a teenage boy's skin,
The bold stigma oozing
Diamond like precum as he
dreams and flowers.

Out, out. They reach out,
not knowing why or what
They are longing for,
Oblivious of their transient
Beauty, the heartbreak of time.

Symbol of spring and Easter
Youth and resurrection.
The lily blossoms and fades
Called by the sun and the earth
To its rise and demise.

Lost

After Frost

The field becomes a sea of
Stars or diamonds, whatever
Cliché image comes to mind
For a magical landscape. The dog,
Oblivious to the stellar turf, treads
Carefully on the spongy grasses
Following the scent of deer or coyote
Who have visited in the night.

Inside, my roommate is lost in the
Blue light of his cell phone, two
Asian lesbians flaming his desire,
He on automatic palm pilot until
His loud anti-climatic sneeze resounds
Through the apartment

And I go to the kitchen to
Contemplate a lonely coffee.

Peony 3

Last Shift

The joy I took earlier Mikey
Was walking out into the field
With our dog and watching the
Stars again. There was a little
Firefly there on the night, trying
To land his plane, and I tried and
Tried to will him down southeast
Where I think the airport is.

The little dipper had disappeared.
I could not find the larger,
Right off the handle I was told,
But, both were gone. I guess the sky rotates in
Winter. I was never much good at astronomy.

Well, I came in. What could I do?
His light had gone out: either
Landed or crashed, or still out
There somewhere hanging on
The black velvet curtain of night
Like a small ruby, or tear.

We'd had our walk,
Night did it's usual
Blessing, and I may now
Sleep, Mikey, Lucky.

Covid Casualty

> "Next time don't wrangle, give the boy the money, Call
> across chasms what the world you know is. Luckless and
> lied to, how can a child master human decorum?
>
> Next time a switchblade, somewhere he is thinking, I
> should have killed him and took the lousy wallet. Reading
> my cards he feels a surge of anger blind as my shame.
>
> Error from Babel mutters in the places,
> Cities apart, where now we word our failures:
> Hatred and guilt have left us without language who
> Might have held discourse."
>
> After a mugging, from *Effort at Speech* by William
> Meredith

The world is in an uproar of protest over the death of
George Floyd. A poet lists grievances from lynchings to
The Tulsa Massacre to the current murders by a police
Force oblivious to its racism.

Meredith understood the original sin of racism,
While some well-meaning people contend it is
Part of our DNA, that if you cannot rewire your genetics,
You should at least insist on justice until our better angels
Begin to permeate our humanity.

How can we train ourselves to love, to avoid vindictiveness
When a roommate who can not breathe, claustrophobic
In the lockdown, takes his chances somewhere else
Abandons you to grief and emptiness?

It is human to hate death, to hate loneliness, to hate the
Different sorts of trouble life hands you in a physical
And moral pandemic. But how to live with this history,
This loss, to create a new world?

Easter

Stretching Out

Post Prandial

I'm hiding a ring for you
Or it could perhaps be a crown –
A friendship ring, say, to
Share a friendship.
Or, a ring of thorns to
Share in spirit, high or
Low what the other
Might be suffering.

A Lenten sort of idea. At one
Point in my life I wanted to follow
Jesus through the act of dying as
He lay there those hours after
His crucifixion and contemplated
Going against the gates of
Hell, or wherever
His disengaged Spirit
Was heading. The
Son of God and
Me hanging out. Oh
Brother, I am with thee.
Are You with me Jesus?

Pioneer Brother, Senior Scout
Show me the way, man. I am
Afraid for us both Brother.
I am only halfway into the light.
Trust, dear God, in my fortitude.

Palm Sunday
for Lizzie

In the fractured forests of New England
Fewer predators like fox or opossum
Who eat the tick-laden mice
Account for the spread of the
Blood-borne disease named for
Lyme, that toney village just down
The pike from me here in Groton.

"It wasn't no fucking bat",
A conspiracy theorist posts
On Facebook, "the Chinese did it
To wipe us all out and now their
Biological weapon has backfired.
We are all going to die," he proclaims,
Which is certainly true ultimately.

But it seems we have to learn
How to live with other animals–
Social distancing on an environmental,
Global scale, not just in our lonely lives
These days when all you can do is
Wave to a neighbor. Still, there is sweet Lizzie
Willing to lend you a few bucks to tide you over.
Nurses put on their masks and go into the
Nursing home like a fireman entering a
Burning building. Bible study classes
Go on picking through the Good Book, debating
What sort of animal Jesus rode into Jerusalem,
The week of His passion. In the end, we are all
Animals hoping to mutate into better angels
Through His final release and resurrection.

Peony 4

Pasen: Vroege Morgen

Een Kleine engel, een scout
beroert Hem. Kom op Vriend.
Je moet opstaan. Er is
werk aan de winkel.

Easter 4:00 AM

A minor angel, His scout
Shakes Him. Come on Buddy
You have to get up now.
You have work to do.

tr. Tom Veys

The Good Old Days

Saturday: Holy Week

> "My name is Ozymandias, king of kings:
> Look on my works, ye Mighty, and despair!'
> Nothing beside remains. Round the decay
> Of that colossal wreck, boundless and bare
> The lone and level sands stretch far away."
> —Percy Bysshe Shelley

I guess the world really will return
To some kind of normal afterwards
The way trees and ferns fanned out in
Primavera glory after the Bubonic Plague.

I'll fly away for sure someday as
Will we all, and what will the world make of
My little spirit which has waked a while
Among others walking this poor burgeoning
Planet?

The day before His resurrection,
What was He thinking, I have always
Wondered, before the angel descended And
Rolled away the great rock keeping Him in
The dark, dreaming of the gates of Hell as
His blood pooled beneath Him?

"Here lies one whose name was writ in
Water," Keats requested for his Tombstone.
In fact, the poems seem writ In blood,
Indelible, despite the fact that He turned to
Ashes there of the Spanish steps.

"Nothing matters," my mother's friend
Pronounced as she lay dying. The dead In
Italy and all over the world would agree.

The mystery of being. Can it possibly end,
Can it possibly matter, this our dark
Rumination as we lie on stone with
Our Brother, waiting for the light.

Epilogue

Face

Camus' Stranger

The priest, trying to give solace
To Camus' stranger, says he
Must believe in an afterlife.
And when the free-floating
Murderer says nothing,
Sure that nothing matters,
The priest incredibly,
Wants to kiss him.

How does it end, we don't know.
The prisoner accepts the guillotine:
The blade is sharp no matter when
It comes slicing down. The prisoner
Reflects, "And what difference could
It make if, after being charged with
Murder, he were executed because
He didn't weep at his mother's funeral?"

Of the priest he says, "Couldn't he grasp
What I meant by that dark wind blowing
From my future?" For the first time the
Stranger lays his heart open to the
"Benign indifference of the universe."

All he asks is that, "On the day of my execution,
There should be a huge crowd of spectators
And that they should greet me with howls of
Execrations." Justice becomes political
Assassination. Murder is murder. Da Vinci
Says it best, "it is an infinitely atrocious act
To take away the life of a man."

But this man, this strange man.
How he lingers at the edge of
What it means to be human,
How he smells and thinks and
Loves. How intriguing he is, and
How glad we are that he lived.

About the Artists

RITA DAWLEY

Rita Dawley is a mixed media artist. Her drawings are quilt like. They include brightly colored, unique childlike images of people, animals and buildings. These images are also incorporated into woodcut prints. Rita attended the Paier School of Art and Connecticut College. She is a member of the Connecticut Academy of Fine Arts, The Norwich Arts Canter Gallery, Mystic Arts Center, Guilford Art League and New Haven Paint and Clay. Rita Dawley lives and works in Uncasville, Connecticut

JUNER ZHAI (JUNER PATNODE)

Juner specializes in traditional Chinese watercolor painting as well as being adept in modern formats and calligraphy. With Chinese watercolor, there are not only two different techniques (Xieyi—which is freehand done quickly and Gongbi—which is meticulous traditional realism) yet each is done with a different kind of rice paper. In each technique there are three styles: Flower and Animal / Landscape / Portrait. As part of the Chinese Cultural Revolution, Juner specializes in the Flower and Animal style yet is also well-versed with Landscape. Juner has been influenced by traditional Chinese Culture and Artists and has also been influenced by exposure to Western Culture and Artists. With private and corporate experience as a designer, Juner has worked as a Trademark Designer for China Packaging Import and Export Co., Ltd. (1998) and Qinghai Trademark Firm (2006). Several of her designs and trademarks have gone onto successful products in the marketplace and her designs have also appeared as book covers and in publications.

She recently married the American artist, Mark Patnode and lives and works in New London, Connecticut

PANCHO MALENZANOV

(cover artist) was born in 1964 and started painting seriously at age 15, when he was accepted into the School for Applied Arts in his hometown Sofia.

"Painting has been always my 'calling'," he says. "In my teenage years I was strongly influenced by the Bulgarian artists Greddy Assa, Roumen Rachev, and Hundertwasser. My first paintings were mostly abstract landscapes, painted with oil and pastel. For me, nature is large part of my inner peace; therefore painting nature brought out my 'self.' I would dare to call them 'flying landscapes'. I see most images in my head from a bird's point of view. Also, for me, the presence and inspiration of a loved one plays an important role, and it is then that I do my best work." Malenzanov also paints "machineries": laptops, airplanes, boats, and submarines, with a special vision on how to incorporate those objects. "Music plays a very important role in my life and work: Jazz gives me a lot, so I feel obligated to 'give back' to jazz through my paintings." He lives and works in Sofia and London.

White Lotus

www.ingramcontent.com/pod-product-compliance
Lightning Source LLC
Chambersburg PA
CBHW040002110526
44587CB00001BA/26